LOVE YOU TO PIECES

BEAUTIFUL MONSTER

Written by J.K. Coy

Follow @StoriesbyJKCoy on Facebook. I'd love to hear what makes your baby a Beautiful Monster!

To Wynn, my very own beautiful monster; your spirit is already so strong.

Your contagious smiles are the purist form of happiness I have ever encountered. I pray you never lose your ability to spread happiness to those of us that need it most.

P.S. You're a bit of a monster.

TO:

FROM:

Every day you make me crazy.

I love you to pieces, Beautiful Monster.

In the middle of the night you woke me,
to let me know you pooped your pants.

I love you to pieces, **Beautiful Monster**.

In the morning I made our family breakfast, while you screamed at me for not giving you ALL of my attention.

I love you to pieces, **Beautiful Monster**.

After breakfast I thought you would have fun with your toys. Instead, you forgot how to hold your pacifier in your mouth and it was all my fault.

I love you to pieces, Beautiful Monster.

This afternoon I finally attempted to shower in peace.
You decided to let me know how awful I was for setting you down.

I love you to pieces, Beautiful Monster.

During your nap, the dog barked at the delivery man. It woke you up and really ruined your day.

I love you to pieces, Beautiful Monster.

Before we left the house I dressed you in the cutest outfit I could find. Apparently, it wasn't as comfortable as your pajamas, and you wanted to let me know.

I love you to pieces, Beautiful Monster.

Dad was gone at work all day and you missed him.
So, you welcomed him home by screaming in his arms.

He loves you to pieces, **Beautiful Monster**.

At the restaurant, we prayed you would be quiet so we could eat dinner at the same time. You slept peacefully…UNTIL our food arrived.

We love you to pieces, **Beautiful Monster**.

After bath time we tried to clip your nails. By your reaction, you would have thought we threw away all your toys!

We love you to pieces, **Beautiful Monster.**

While Mom and Dad tried to relax and catch up, you reminded us that all conversations were supposed to revolve around you.

Yeah.

We love you to pieces, **Beautiful Monster**.

We got you all cozy for bed, but then you decided you were
too hot...*or* too cold...*or* too hungry...*or* too full...*or* too excited...
...*or* too TIRED...to go to sleep.

I'm not tired...just resting

my eyes...

Ok.

Deeep breathe…

We love you to pieces, Beautiful Monster.

Then all of a sudden you STOP.

You look into my eyes and grin from ear to ear.

You finally close your eyes,
and angelically fall asleep in my arms.

And it's my turn to tear up.

I freaking LOVE YOU to pieces, Beautiful Monster.

ABOUT THE AUTHOR

J.K. Coy is a first-time Mom that doesn't sit still well. She holds a Bachelor's in Business and a Master's in Elementary Education. During the brief moments between her roles as a corporate climber, Mom and Wife, she enjoys sharpening her creative pencil.

Her intent is to entertain the parent and child at the same time. Sometimes it's the little joys, and inside jokes, that get everyone through another bedtime routine.

Follow her on Facebook @StoriesbyJKCoy for the latest details on new releases (and how she's managing her own Beautiful Monster).